When Dymond Speaks

By

Dymond Horton

 **Love__Dymond**

https://www.youtube.com/@whendymondspeaks8008

DEDICATION

To all the little black girls
and mature black women
who were told no.
No you can't do something,
no you won't be something...
You can and you will!
Because now we're breaking
statistics and destroying
stereotypes formed against us.

"You may shoot me with your words,
you may cut me with your eyes,
you may kill me with your hatefulness,
But still, like air, I'll rise"
-Maya Angelou

INTRODUCTION

After being in charter school and private school growing up, in middle school it was time to embrace the real world. Unshielded, unsugarcoated, and unapologetic public school. Here I was, facing all the challenges of a preteen girl in a new environment.
I didn't have the best coping skills but one thing I could do was write!
I started writing poetry, and even songs about all the things I saw and experienced.
I am a heterosexual black woman, I am Gen Z, I am a Christian; I struggle with anxiety, and more recently I've overcome permanent hearing loss, in one ear, by receiving a cochlear implant. Now at 17, I can say I have come through some mountains and some valleys.
How do you stand on everything you are, in a world of adversity?
After performing one of my pieces following the tragic murder of Ahmaud Arbery in 2020, I realized that my work touched many.
My voice, my pain, my questions sent shock waves throughout my community because so many people felt the same way!
So in this collection, I bare my soul. My demons, my uncertainty... a vulnerability where I have never found comfort before now; and it is for the sake of the reader who lives with doubt or fear. The little black girls who struggle to find their place in the world or their voice in the community.
Speak your truth and love yourself.
Never stop fighting and trust that you will find your way.

@Love__Dymond

TABLE OF CONTENTS

TABLE OF CONTENTS

PROTESTS!

I.CANT.BREATHE

I.CANT.BREATHE

George Floyd

Breonna Taylor

Ahmaud Arbery

Sandra Bland

Freddie Grey

Trayvon Martin

Tamir Rice

There are seven too many names on that list

At this point going *#OutsideWhileBlack*

is a huge risk but even inside her house,

Breonna took her last breath, and she'll be missed.

We live in a world where for just being black

you could get stopped and at least frisked

So let me explain, why

"Power to the people" goes way further than our fists

Because if you don't stand for something,

you fall for everything

White officers, just married to the job and the cuffs

near the hand of a black man is the wedding ring

You think these United States were built for U and not US.

But United starts with U N I

We tell our young black men

"Be respectful to the officer. Comply"

But even the ones who did that didn't come home alive.

and there's a u IN us and you don't seem

to understand that

and for you to treats us like humans,

we can't even demand that

We have to prove to you that we're living humans,

flesh and blood

And not animals, criminals, drug dealers,

hustlers, killers, or thugs

I'm sick of it

I'm sick of Black Mother's having to worry about if they're

sons will make it home safe

Worried that they'll get stopped and ultimately

killed due to their race?

You gotta make a change and it gotta start today

We gotta make a change and we gotta pick up the pace

My mom had to have "The Talk"

with my brother and he's only six

Don't you think that's tragic?

Had the talk in hope later that night

he comes back through the do'

So he don't end up like Emit Till "don't beat me no mo"

So he don't end up like Trayvon

"what is you following me fo'"

Why is it that you're so bothered?

Why is it that you decide to murder innocent daughters,

sons, mothers, and fathers?

Is it our nappy hair that provokes you?

Our deeply rooted heritage that wraps a

round your neck and chokes you?

...I can't breathe

AND NEITHER COULD GEORGE FLOYD

WHEN YOU HELD HIM DOWN WITH YOUR KNEE

Over heating and losing breath, brought about a nosebleed

But this is America, home of the brave, land of the free?

You keep saying

"We wouldn't have a problem

if you'd protest peacefully"

But

WE WOULDN'T HAVE A PROBLEM

IF YOU'D JUST TREAT US EQUALLY

You wonder why we riot, protest, and loot

But at this point, you won't even cooperate with

"Hands up, Don't Shoot"

All lives don't matter until black lives do

You could NEVER understand

what it is that we're going through

All it takes is for me to be African American.

Check.

So here's my question;

Am I next?

Are you next?

Who's Next?

WHEN RIOTS BECOME DEADLY

When Riots Become Deadly

America is going down in the dirt

We thought it would get better with the new decade,

it's getting worse.

The madness just doesn't stop unless someone is in a hearse

and even after that, they walk around with

"Keeping America Great"

on their shirts Trump didn't get his way

Now all the "United" States have to pay

They wanna start a riot near inauguration day

But not nearly as many of them died as the

black people last May.

The people who stormed the Capitol getting arrested

But the ones put TO REST are the blacks who peacefully

protested.

Someone wake me up from this awful dream

where white people can threaten

the nation then go home and make memes

How much more racist could it get?

Y'all climbing a building for a man who

LET'S NOT FORGET

Wants an entire wall built to keep out-

a whole race of people... yet he's still in the white house.

After two tries to get him impeached

He was still acquitted and influencing the police

and those who weren't on his side,

got beat with american flags

Where were the rubber bullets and the tear gas?

Feds found a truck full of bombs nearby

But cops kill the black men, even ones who comply

They slowly arrested those who

thought the Capitol building

was appropriate to climb

While they shot black people because

they felt threatened by voices and signs

Tell me Trump not racist when those fighting for him carried

confederacy and I bet Ahmaud's killers thought what they

did was okay because of this presidency on top of all that,

I seen women out there throwing flags and bottles

When in 2015 "grab 'em by the coochie" was his motto

Nancy Pelosi was almost taken

hostage and had a stolen computer

and a rioter said he wanted to run her over or shoot her

The NAACP tweeted best

They've killed us for less

rioters had zip ties to hold people hostage.

All because of a decision whether to replace

Trump, promoted great losses

We're not asking that you kill them the same

We're asking that you STOP killin because it's insane

Black people were such a threat that they deserved

to die because of their peaceful choices

But the white people literally made

harmful threats with their voices

No matter how much we say

"Hands Up, Don't Shoot"

That don't seem to be true

because as much as we surrender,

shooting is EXACTLY what they do

and I just think it's disproportional, how about you?

REVENGE vs REPARATIONS

REVENGE vs REPARATIONS

What would you prefer? Revenge or reparations?

Maybe you need more context, you need to know the situation

let's put it like this, if you were uprooted from your nation

and forced into labor, manual and birth due to forced sexual relations

would you want your compensation?

Or would you want your get back on any and every occasion?

White people claim we all like to steal but they stole us

so for us to occasionally take back from them, is it a must?

Or should we politely ask for our money

nah because when we passive, they laughin' like something's funny.

They had us afraid and chasing a star to get freed

and still haven't given us the means for everything we need

yet they're born into generational wealth

maybe we should take everything they have and keep it for ourselves

for revenge, maybe we should plan an election

and tell them they can't go

or kidnap them and make them work in the caves of the Cango

maybe we should speak in a way they don't understand

like "they don't know our slang 'doe"

or maybe we should fight back

like Jamie Foxx in Django you know,

whipping them till blood leaks

holding them hostage and starving them for weeks

we could separate them from their kin

and take their dignity whenever we desire and then

free them only by order of the authority men

and then let them know they're only 60% of a person

oh and now you're not finding this amusing

but it was pure entertainment when it was your doing

when you owned slaves in southern cities

and Harriet had to run and whisper

"if you wanna live, come with me"

you took out fathers, our lives

our husbands, our wives

you put welts and holes in our backs

all because we are black

everything you took from us, we want it back

...or do we?

God gave me life and the means to survive and do me

so that I don't have to wait for you to give it to me

and as for the revenge,

God wouldn't want us to be vengeful so you can keep that, truly

but do I hope you get what you deserve?

Absolutely

I want you all to feel how we felt

to take the cards you dealt

to feel so chained up and you

can't get free and you have no help

to feel so outta place in a country YOU BUILT

that you understand why Kaepernick knelt

the Bible says you reap what you sow

so for all the times you told us no

i hope your lifestyle gets uprooted, everything you know

then you'll understand

what we were hollering fo'

WHAT ARE YOU THANKFUL FOR?

WHAT ARE YOU THANKFUL FOR

I woke up this morning with a thankful attitude

Because today is a day that we love to show gratitude

a day to tell you what I appreciate about you and

not why I'm mad at you

So I can say I'm grateful for what I have and for what I'm lackin' too

Thankful that I never caught that deadly disease

Thankful that I wasn't another death that

brought my family to their knees

Thankful that I didn't struggle too much although money

don't grow on trees and thankful that I love my family and that

they're thankful for me. Even when nothing seems to be going right

I'm thankful for new breaths every morning and another chance at life

I know things get ugly and situations get tight

but I thank God that last night wasn't my last night

Y'all why do we feel like today is the one to feel blessed?

The only day a year when we try not to acknowledge our stress

One day for us to go have a celebratory feast and make a mess

Because if we're thankful everyday why now should it be expressed

We make such a big production about boiling

greens and slaughtering turkey

Just like the Europeans did the Native Americans

but "hey, Christopher Columbus didn't hurt me"

Most times we pray over the feast,

thank God and make it churchy

But imitating an apologetic feast for genocide

just makes me feel dirty

I mean how would you feel today

if monsters came and annexed your whole residence.

If they killed your whole family and community and set

all new precedents.

The few of you that survived got a dinner and some

negligence.

Then they said they discovered the land you had first, even

with obvious evidence. We would never be accepting of these

circumstances.

And we all wanna be woke but show oblivion to these

stances.

By enjoying the dinner and all the holiday's romances

And don't say you don't celebrate because you work if it's only for the

holiday bonus and pay advances I mean come on

I say give thanks whenever we feel appreciative

Maybe come up with our own celebration be innovative

Give thanks for life and love

at a time when it's not debated and not in

mimicry of when the

Europeans stole the lives and land of the Natives.

WHY WE COUNT

WHY WE COUNT

Before we're not configured into the count,

consider this

If we're not accounted for,

we don't exist

Especially age group 13-18

and where we live

What about our free school lunches

or

the snap benefits the government gives?

Our environment will become a ghost town,

and from there, everything will just slowly go down.

What will happen to our spirited school sports teams?

Or our local neighborhood chill spot for ice cream?

And what about our library with books that we use for free?

I know being skipped over wouldn't benefit me.

Everything works here like a community

and no matter how many flaws we have, we still have unity

So if we have the option to be counted, we should choose to be

Because we're important too and our high school that is soon to be.

Is it okay for our school district to fail?

Because the government wants to put more money in the jail?

And what about our playgrounds and local pool fun?

We need to be taken into account, and tallied.

Everyone

THIS is why we count.

STEREOTYPES

STEREOTYPES

So now you join an equality club and think you're an activist

You seriously wanna get hired but now a high school graduate

It's really really sad that it even had to come down to this

Oh my God!!

You going against racism, profiling, and police brutality

But behind closed doors you killin yo own, this is reality

Can't wear a colored scarf in public, it's the hood mentality

Just because you wear that color they shoot. Got the audacity?

Back in the day they made us work for free, manual labor

But nowadays you can't even get a job.

Do me a favor?

Pull up ya' pants, fix ya' collar. That's what they pay attention to.

You try to get a job, they dismiss you before the interview.

We got it hard being black, yo. The hatred and the despise.

Shout out to the Central Park five and Korey Wise

Not like the other guys.

Only there for support and we here today in and outta court

Man quit goin' to jail. How you help your family?

Gotcha 'baby momma' workin' 2, 3 jobs.

This is a tragedy.

You think you get all these chances? No, man this is insanity.

You get one chance to get it right, then you're in the system.

Police shot a man,

thought a brush was a gun, now po po po the victim.

No I'm not dissing you,

just giving words of wisdom.

Don't give in to the stereotypes. It'll ruin your life.

They can't wait to call you an animal because you got in a fight

They called us monkeys and that n-word, and you here repeating it.

Can't find anything else to say?

It's like the insult...hmmm... you're needing it.

You should be a part of a

movement-matter of fact- you should be leading it.

Instead of calling each other that, you should be defeating it.

Yes, the world can get outta hand. But it's all according to God's plan.

So don't try to change destiny and end another life man.

AS A BLACK WOMAN

AS A BLACK WOMAN

Oh say can you see

the welts on my back from slavery

during this anthem I take a knee

because why represent a country that don't represent me

yes, I live in America and there's no pride about it

I'm a black woman in the US so your image of me is

probably clouded I'm at a disadvantage unlike a white man

by whom this country was founded because I'm black they

kidnapped me and brought me here on a boat

as a woman even after everyone else, I couldn't vote

because I'm black they say three-fifths of a person

as a woman that say I'm not strong enough to be workin

because I'm black I value nice things so I must've been

raised in the trap as a woman and I don't earn the same

amount, I suffer a pay gap black woman; they say I'm loud

and obnoxious but it's just passion black woman; they say I

got too much hips and thighs and body to fit in with ideal

fashion black woman; they say I can't be in charge, a man is who I must be backing black woman; because I'm not

worthy of being a title, maybe a caption

Malcolm X said that in America

the black woman is the most disrespected

the black woman is the most unprotected

the black woman is the most neglected

so as a black woman, your incivility is to be expected

as a black woman, the odds are against me

they expect me to seek validation in the

wrong place because I feel dumb or ugly

then I'll end up dropping out because I'm busy with a baby

then I'm uneducated so unemployed so then my wallet is empty

but I have faith that we can keep beating the odds

that we can soar above the expected while we walk with God

faith has brought us this far and we haven't fallen yet

so let's keep believing in the life we can't see until all our

goals are met as a black woman I walk by

faith and not by sight because I know

I'm made in the

image of God

at the end of the night

but as a black woman,

I pray that

we keep beating the odds

and what

THEY SAY in the land of the

somewhat free while

black womanhood

is the home of the brave

SEE MY COLOR

SEE MY COLOR

Most people think that they can fix racism with a simple phrase

" I dont see color"...

"What's the difference" they say

They pretend they cant see the brown complexion

my parents made

but no;

see my color!

Open your eyes, remove the shades.

Because

Black is beautiful,

Black is who I am

Black is me, openly,

not hiding it like its a scam

Just because you want to ignore it when I walk through your

neighborhood

Woah...now let me slow down and not get too angry,

not start a war

Because then you'll see the angry blackness

that was invisible to you before.

We never asked you to pretend we werent black.

We just dont want you to treat us bad because of that

and for you to treat us equally because of that simple fact

Because why should you have to defend yourself,

if seeing my color wasnt so bad?

I love the color of me and my braidable, nappy hair and

of my cousins who vary in color or my ethicity

But its not me that you dont wanna see,

you don't wanna see our history

if you don't see my color--when

you look at me

==you see invisibility.

But you rather disregard my skin tone

because of your inability to accept our difference.

To acknowledge my innocence

Because when you see a brown shade you see guilty

Your ancestors saw dirty, worthless, slave, filthy.

Whether you see my color or not, this is how

God built me so take off your

negro neglectors.

Remove your

melanin rejectors

and acknowledge my color,

just interpret it better

LEGACY

LEGACY

I wanna be remembered and leave a mark

and do something great so when you hear my name,

you feel that spark

I wanna have an impact on the lives of many

and leave a good impression, a great one if any

I want my people to see that they can be what they wanna be

and that they can travel and see what they wanna see

I wanna leave an imprint like Dr. King

and show people what he meant when he said "let freedom ring"

I might wanna draw up a bill or invent a new thing

and show my little black girls they can fly,

if they would just realize they have wings

I wanna show my young black boys

that they can be whatever they desire

That their origin shouldn't determine

whether or not they get hired

And not to let anything take away their abilities to be inspired

Because they can fly too,

with their jetpacks, they just gotta start the fire

Like Nelson Mandela, I won't let my opposition

take my mind and my heart

Even with my limited freedom,

future generations will still know

my mind is a work of art

God gave me gifts to use them for a purpose

So I'll continue to use them

in schools, home, public events, and churches

I can't be the first Black President, hats off to Barack

and he left a legacy.

So he deserves his props

I can't be the first black woman astronaut,

credit to Mae Jemison

and Kamala Harris already made her way to the

Whitehouse, as a lawyer, arguing whether

people were guilty or innocent

But you see where I'm going with it

I have lots of ideas, a choice won't come instant

But imma be remembered, for doing something different

I wanna write 'Dymond was here' and it have a meaning

and I got big dreams but I don't wanna

wake up and be dreaming

I wanna leave a legacy

So people remember the best of me

In 50 years when you speak my name from memory

When you hear of my works, and all my deeds

I pray you see God, but remember me

JUNETEENTH 2021

JUNETEENTH 2021

I pledge allegiance to the Juneteenth flag that you probably didn't know was a thing

Allegiance and loyalty to the flag that let slaves be free to learn & live, dance & sing

The flag that has a star to represent Texas where they were announced free

and a burst beyond the star that symbolizes new beginnings

I pledge devotion to the arch that means a

new horizon; promise & opportunities

and to the colors that show African Americans

are too Americans and celebrate unity

My people weren't free in 1776, at least the ones who were alive

Instead they were enslaved until Freedom Day in 1865

and some of them weren't even

free then matter-of-fact

Because although they were emancipated the

slave owners didn't tell them that

So through blood sweat and tears they worked through the harvest

All because when comparing skin, there's was the darkest.

My melanin don't define me and nor did it define my ancestors

They thought we were lesser and we took care of land better

So yup we deserve reparations if you ask me

How they forced us to do their work

because we're black is pretty nasty!

But think about how my people represent for each other and do it pretty gladly

The effort we put into our black excellence is pretty past me

How we just ran for Ahmaud and rioted for

Breonna last year, but still feel it like it was last week

and how we go through a lot but live by believing

"God can defeat anything trying to attack me"

On this Black Independence Day we celebrate how our people are creators

How we set trends for the nation and don't have a problem

stepping in the face of haters

and how we now step in name of love

with the same feet that once bore craters

and how we were smart enough to escape slavery

but I'll get to that later

Step dancing routines are something else we tend to create

We bare expression through our feet and

we started stepping to communicate

When we step, we step loud for people to hear us

Maybe we step to keep the modern day

slave owners from coming near us

Maybe we're so afraid that we step for you to fear us

We never back down

Here in Sandusky, we celebrate the underground

railroad that happened right beneath us

and Harriet Tubman who helped free us

and the people here in Sandusky who aided slaves

in their Canada travels

To freedom through Zion Baptist Church in 1849

and underground channels

They say about 3,000 miles of underground

railroad tracks existed in Ohio

So now I feel obligated to wave this flag

everywhere I go

Jesus said "I in them and you in me---

So that they may be brought to complete unity.

Then the world will know that you sent me and have

loved them just as you have loved me"

Read that in John 17:23 in case you ever wonder

how wrong was slavery

I pledge Allegiance to Juneteenth flag that

represents the day my people were finally free

JUNETEENTH 2023

JUNETEENTH 2023

I pledge allegiance to the Juneteenth flag that you probably didn't

know was a thing Allegiance and loyalty to the flag

that let slaves be free to learn & live, dance & sing.

The flag that has a star to represent Texas

where they were announced free

and a burst beyond the star that symbolizes

new beginnings I pledge devotion to the

arch that means a new horizon;

promise & opportunities and

to the colors that show African Americans

are too Americans and celebrate unity.

My people weren't free on July 4th 1776,

at least the ones who were alive

Instead they were enslaved until Freedom Day in 1865

They were actually free 2 years prior matter-of-fact

Because although they were emancipated

the slave owners didn't tell them that

So through blood sweat and tears they

worked through the harvest

43.

All because when comparing skin, there's was the darkest

Our melanin shouldn't put us at a disadvantage

like it did our ancestors

They looked at us like subordinates and we took

care of land better

So yeah family we deserve reparations if you ask me

How they forced us to do their labor

because we're black is pretty nasty

But think about how my people represent

for each other and do it pretty gladly.

The effort we put into our black excellence

and make it look classy

How we ran for Ahmaud and rioted for Breonna in 2020,

but still feel it like it was last week

and how we suffer through a lot but believe

"God can defeat anything trying to attack me"

On this Black Independence Day

we celebrate how our people are creators

How we set trends for the nation

and don't have a problem stepping in the face of haters

and how we now step in name of love

with the same feet that once bore craters

and we're smart enough to escape slavery

but I'll get to that later.

Step dancing routines are something

my folks tend to create

We don't step to scare

people we used to step to communicate

When they refuse to hear our voice,

we step to overcompensate

And we step fast to be on time

but to freedom we was two years late

When we step, we step loud for people to hear us

Maybe we step to keep the modern day slave owners from

coming near us

Maybe we're so afraid that we step for you to fear us

So as a step in the right direction

I wrote us a letter, so DEAR US

It's time to walk in our purpose,

any obstacle is ready to tackle

We no longer need permission,

our freedom is most of the battle

We got that dawg in us, that fight, it's natural

So I'm done dragging my feet because

they're no longer in shackles

Jesus said

"I in them and you in me---

So that they may be brought to complete unity.

Then the world will know

that you sent me and have loved

them just as you have loved me"

Read that in John 17:23

in case you ever wonder how sinful was slavery

I pledge Allegiance to Juneteenth flag that represents

the day my people were free.

STRUGGLES
AS A
WOMAN

47.

TRAPPED: SEX TRAFFICKING

TRAPPED: SEX TRAFFICKING

"Just a few more questions, then you're free to leave,"

the officer told me.

But where do I go? Home?

Back where I was

secretly lonely?

Back before he tricked me and then, took me, and

then sold me?

Or back in those rooms when the men took

advantage?

Or when my captor tried to fix my scars,

he made, with a bandage?

I mean,

Is home where I was

when he used me for gain

like an object?

Or on the corner where I had to work

for my freedom like a contest?

Is home with my four children,

taken from me at birth?

Sometimes it feels like

home is nowhere on this earth

Is home in the hand

of the man that

grabbed me by my curves?

Or chained up with

over 20 million victims that

are scared and diverse?

Will I ever have a home where I feel safe

without looking over my shoulder?

A home where life doesn't weigh

so heavy like boulders

I want to know, where exactly is my home?

An expression for where I would reside alone.

But the only place I can think of is the love that

God has shown

He brought me out the mess and made

sure I was alive and he gave me a home

where I would not only survive, but thrive

Home is my sane place

with God in my mind

and maybe my perception of

physical home

will get better with time

But because of him

I'm standing here today

and it's a way better day than yesterday

I'm stronger than ever and that's all I gotta say

Because I'm a Queen, I'm free, and I'm okay

WHAT NOW GOD?
I GOT SOME QUESTIONS

WHAT NOW GOD? I GOT SOME QUESTIONS

Dear God,

I know you know it's me and I know you know what I'm here for

because I've heard that you see everything and

maybe I should open my ears more

but I don't wanna believe that you were present that day.

I don't wanna think you could hear, Lord

I wanna keep it buried but it just keeps

POPPING back up, like a cold sore

I just wanna know, if you were there,

why would you let that happen to me

Some people say that's it's so I can be stronger,

but all I feel is weak

this situation got me staying up some nights

because I can't sleep

feeling like I'm not worth as much as someone else may see

and now after 6 years, I'm in a state of confusion, praying on my knees

Because I need answers as to why I can't just be free

Free of these thoughts, these flashbacks, these insecurities

Free of the fact that I can't confidently walk down the street

Lord, I wanna know why'd you let him do it?

Why'd you let me walked around feeling as though I'm ruined

Like I could never be good enough for anybody, not even myself

Got me saying things in the mirror that I'd never even say to

somebody else

Feeling as though it doesn't matter where I go from here

Because now I'm dirty, unclean, not innocent; nowhere near

Now I'm acting careless and not preserving my body

All because of the fact that he couldn't keep his hands off me

Were my attempted screams not enough to say I don't want it?

Or because I was comfortable in my own home did he feel taunted?

Did it seem like I was showing off? Like "if you got it, flaunt it"

Because as a nine-year-old girl, that is not what I was doing. Honest

Sometimes I feel like...God, help me understand

Why couldn't you just make me a man?

So he couldn't do what he did, why was this part of the plan?

How is this gonna change me for the better,

because all it's made me is worse

All it has done is make me try to cope with and cover up the hurt

It's made me so afraid that I wanna keep defense in my purse

And it made me feel so dirty that sometimes I feel like I won't

even be accepted in the church.

God I don't think you were punishing me to

benefit a pervert and maybe this wasn't you at all,

and it's all just the devil's work

HANDS OFF

HANDS OFF

According to my schools dress code, off the shoulder is too revealing

showing too much skin is too appealing

too many holes in your jeans and boys get to staring and boys

get to feeling.

So many restrictions but nobody cares about our feelings

Maybe it's just hot so I don't wanna wear full sleeves,

or maybe I got a really cute shirt that I want my friends to see

Maybe I find it cute to have holes in my jeans

Whatever the case is I'm not telling the boys to look at me

I can't wear certain shorts or crop top shirts

I'm expected to dress like a lady but when I wear skirts

I get complaints about those because someone thinks they're short

But conveniently we can wear

volleyball spandex for the school sports

Cheerleaders can wear little skirts on the courts and the field

During basketball and football season when the air

would the most chilled but anything for school spirit, right

It doesn't matter how short the skirts are when

they're chanting "go-team-go" lyrics, right?

During rape prevention week at school they stay on top of things

They tell us girls we can't do a lot of things

Don't wear skirts

Don't wear low cut v-neck shirts

Don't expose your shape

Don't walk home alone late

How about hey guys, don't rape...

They make it easy for the blame to be on the girls

Blame it on the clothes we wear but how in the world

Can you blame me for a boy taking advantage

When he's responsible for emotional baggage

and physical damage

All because of me wearing a shirt that he thought was romantic

I just think we should make them take accountability

and that's the cause of all this hostility

It just doesn't make sense that sometimes

I can't dress for the weather

Because the school system doesn't wanna do better

And this isn't a new thing, it's been like this forever

And I just think they should get it together

ABORTION:
AN ONGOING CONVERSATION

ABORTION: AN ONGOING CONVERSATION

Hi, my name is abortion
I'll share with you the description of what I do, or maybe just a portion
I get rid of some people's problems also known as unwanted kids
I help people dust their hands off and think it is what it is

Hold on wait is that really how it goes?
I get an abortion and sweep the dust from my soles?

I might break up a family or leave someone depressed
But hey, no screaming toddlers so you can get some rest

Some rest sounds pretty good, cuz I work hard every night!
But I don't want depression, what does the process look like?

I poke at the baby or cancel them with a suction
And depending on my type you could get a price reduction

I damage women's bodies and leave possible health issues
But at least they have no snotty nose kids that'll need a tissue

Wait its not all about me, I mean I'm not THAT
in love with my hips. And why'd you have to mention bratty kids?
I say no thank you and everybody flips

Right...
Because that's just life

I can just eradicate an unborn child, without a fight
As long as you can have unprotected sex all over again, tonight

See now you trying to play me, don't judge me let me choose

Sure, the declaration gives humans the right to happiness, life, and liberty
But come to the clinic and the right to life is taken by mystery

And let me guess, it ALWAYS leads to misery.

No I can be beneficial too
I can take the baby if the conception was untrue
If you don't want the product that a rapist gave you
I'll kill it for a price and you're good as new

Yea I know some young girls who have to fight this trauma

And YOU could take away that pain,

if you weren't surrounded by so much drama

But not really though
Just because there's no proof doesn't mean you won't know
It doesn't mean the damage from a brutal rape won't show
But it's true, you won't have a kid to make you feel so low
Except I'll do that for you anyway
I'll leave you with physical and emotional pain
Statistics say I'll leave you with a void
that you might fill with drugs, but hey

Well can't you see how hard it is?

Sometimes I have to numb the pain.

What does the world offer a black baby? What does my child have to gain?

68% of our homes have no fathers, so we work three jobs

to keep the lights on, maybe. No time for me to teach them,

no I can't tuck them in, nobody family

around to help with them, I just cannot win

You might not have been able to find a nanny you could afford to pay
Maybe you wouldn't be financially stable
And adoption probably wasn't on the table
Am I correct?
The option to use me, abortion, was the best.

I don't know nothing about adoption.
I have no help with those papers, and no computer skills.
All I know is I have 3 kids
already and somebody has to pay these bills.

For years we had no right to choose and now I can be free.
So forgive me Lord, please but I'm doing this for me.

I get it, but everyone won't
Some people will tell you don't

They'll tell you there's another way out
But you won't hear what they suggest, no matter how loud
You'll use me to kill your unborn child

Nobody understands me,
and I don't know what else to do so just leave me alone

Hi, my name is abortion
How do you feel about me now?

PRAYER FOR BREAST CANCER

PRAYER FOR BREAST CANCER

Dear God,

I have come to you today lifting my sisters in your name

Thankful that they're strong enough to push through the pain

Thanking you for the gift of medical

care that can pinpoint their problem

and for treatment that can help even if they don't solve 'em

We thank you that these champions are still

here throughout this ongoing cycle

and for the eternal life promised

to those who believe, in the Bible.

We're here appreciating everything you've done

and that you love and care for them

even when they feel numb

I pray that you give these champions the heart and the mind

to believe that they're going to be fine

I pray you give them self control to keep their moods stable

and you give them relief when pain and stress come to the table

I pray that you remind them of the family and friends that have

and of the precious moments that make

them smile and make them laugh

I ask that you remind them daily that they're strong

And that they're conquerors even when things go wrong

And that they seek your word, your hands, and your face

Especially on their bad days

These and other blessings we give thanks

So in the name of Jesus, on behalf of these survivors,

I pray...

Amen

MENTAL

HEALTH

BEEN BLOCKED (EROSION)

BEEN BLOCKED (EROSION)

It's been a minute

I haven't been writing. I wanted to, but I didn't

I was writing all the time then suddenly I stopped

I wanted to get back to it but suddenly I was blocked

I should've been inspired 'cause I've experience a lot

But when I got a pen & paper it's just like my mind locked

Everyone keeps asking me when imma get back to it

Telling me to just jump back in and do it

and you'd think it would be easy because I've been through it

But I couldn't even sit down and write when my life was in ruins

I said "but Ma, if I write about this they might not accept me"

I was acting as though everyone is perfect except me

Everyone has downfalls, this has been my biggest one yet

So here are some things I need to get off my chest

I lost me and neglected my worth

and forgot that there's a purpose that God put me on this earth

I couldn't see my own value and searched for validation

Looked for approval in all the wrong places

I made some bad choices, displayed some bad behavior

and when I decided to fix it, I took that up with the Savior

When I decided to value myself and to do better

Someone also reminded me that I too am

beautifully pieced together

So I started praying and reading the Bible

and I stopped making personal validation my idol

I made sure to fix some relationships and make things right

and grow my relationship with God because he'll always

be there at the end of the night

and with all that, I'm in ninth grade now

I gotta get up, forget my feelings, and work hard

even when the sky's grey now

I gotta put everything to the side and keep getting my A's now

and when I'm feeling down, I just gotta stop and pray now

So this is my comeback. I'm breaking through my block

There's more to come, be prepared to be shocked

I'm journeying with my gift, given by God, who's my rock

So buckle your seatbelts, I'm about to knock your socks...off

ATTACKING ANXIETY

ATTACKING ANXIETY

They told me I had some severe anxiety

I assume the worst and feel like everyone is eyeing me

What symptoms affect me, well there's a variety

But I should be 'normal" according to society

They made me feel alright because

it's common in my age group

But I had to find a beat to complain to

Because I kinda find it hard to remain cool

When I've had the type of dreams that I wish never came true

Thoughts race in my head and I get panic attacks

They be about what I'll lose and about what I lack

About the paths that I chose, and if they're good or bad

Or the target on my back 'cause I'm a woman and black

I get hot and emotional and don't know how to deal

awake from nightmares, crying unable to chill

Often I lose my appetite and don't finish my meal

Battling anxiety ain't something easy to heal

It's even harder when you got other problems

Like attachment issues, don't know how to solve 'em

When people go I'm feeling like I hit rock bottom

Like I have no value unless I got 'em

During attacks, it get hard to breathe

Got me stuttering through my tears like

"uh-huh-please don't leave"

Thinking about those who left and how I'll retrieve

Forgetting I got God and he's all I need

They say "stand against the wall and countdown 10 to 1"

But i just wipe away my tears and then another flood comes

They gave me medication that works for some

But now I can't speak on my feelings as if I was dumb

I gotta express myself so I write or sing

Attacks about attachment holding on by a string

I try and distract myself and think about other things

But i guess this is part of what having anxiety brings.

LETTER FROM #25

LETTER FROM #25

Take me back to the court

where I can run, shoot, and score

and I don't have to worry no more

take me back to the court

where I can defend and steal

where I can get so hungry for success

that winning becomes a meal

where determination is the only emotion I feel

where all my doubts and fears become unreal

because of my adrenaline levels being so surreal

if you love a sport then you know what I mean

like when you do it for yourself and for your team

where you'll get winded on the court

but forget about a bad dream

BREONNA TAYLOR

KOREY WISE

JAYLAND WALKER

ELIHAH MCCLAIN

AHMAUD ARBERY

#SAYMYNAME BREONNA TAYLOR

#SAYMYNAME BREONNA TAYLOR

You've probably heard my story by now, or at least my name

But it's not like I did anything for the fame

Now I'm gone and we have Louisville police to blame

Because they came in shooting blindly like a video game

But you know that already, you know about my death

You already know how I was put to rest

What you don't know about is all the great things I left

So let me get a few things off my chest

Before I had a tragic death I had a great life

I had a great boyfriend who would've made me his wife

What I didn't know was that he had already picked the rock

And I was also an EMT during COVID saving lives on the clock

I aspired to be a nurse one day soon

And my mom said that I'd always light up a room

Speaking of mom's, I wanted to be one too

I had baby names picked out for when that wish came true

Family was everything to me, my sister was my best friend on earth

But they took that away from me during their no-knock search

When they thought drug dealing was happening

in my home with someone from my history

and they shot at the wrong Black and called it

mistaken identity

but that doesn't give them an excuse for what

they did to me

There you go!

That's my life that hasn't been in

the news

Because it's my death that's gotten a lot of views

I know you've heard this before, but that's

because it's major

Arrest the cops that killed

Breonna Taylor.

#SAYMYNAME KOREY WISE

#SAYMYNAME KOREY WISE

The oldest of exonerated five

Korey Wise. Korey. Korey. Korey.

It all started on July 26, 1974 in New York City.

He was born to his mother Dolores and his sisters Marcy and Vanity.

They were both born men.

Koreys dad (who is not named) died way back then.

In 1996 when the cancer ate him.

They say a "high school dropout" is Korey's highest qualification.

But what chances did he have with his allegations?

He had a learning disability and hearing problems were always a challenge.

Deaf, black, mentally objected, and accused. How do you balance?

The Central Park boys were accused of raping a white woman in the park.

They allegedly "knocked her out, and took advantage of her in the dark"

But there was no DNA and the evidence didn't match.

She was in a coma for 12 days, it wasn't just a scratch.

Accused just because they were black.

Five boys in a park, but Korey went back to his significant other.

And they didn't acquire an alibi, they could've asked his lover or his

mother.

Korey only went to the station to accompany his friend.

So, he shouldn't have been there in the end.

He got the worst punishment as he was the oldest of the five.

5-15 years, they said. What a dreadful life?

He was beaten in jail, transferred many times...

The crazy thing is, he didn't commit any of the crimes.

After all the movement, he was taken to one of the

"safest places."

There he met Mattias Reyes, the real rapist.

Korey and Matias fought, then became friends as time progressed.

Until a miracle happen, Matias confesses.

So Korey was released with wicked memories.

He missed out on 14 years. Prison brought so much misery.

They sued NYC and Korey got the biggest portion.

As if money could fix his great misfortune.

"They said if I was there and if I went along with it,

that I could go home. That's all I want it, was to go home.

That's all I still want."

-Korey Wise

#SAYMYNAME JAYLAND WALKER

#SAYMYNAME JAYLAND WALKER

Ain't no cute intro this time because this getting repetitive

done with the gimmicks and subliminals

because they not getting what the message is

ain't no changes been made to the system so here's me, again,

checking it so this goes for the Supreme Court,

the police force, the legislative branch and the rest of it

I mean 90 bullets are you for real?

how could you- why would you-

there ain't even words to describe the anger I

feel y'all trick us into thinking something gon'

get better but then reopen the wound before it heal

so if you want me to care about legal civility you can kiss my...

nevermind

because unlike your weapon I gotta keep that concealed

a broken taillight and a dead lightbulb on the plate

and no criminal record but it became a high speed chase

I mean it was 12:30am, y'all didn't have

no in progress calls or didn't need to be in an actual dangerous place?

Get mad at us for screaming "defund the police" but our tax dollars

paying for unwarranted death.

That's time AND money going to waste

and of course the police gave the same story they give everytime

they feel like they heard a gunshot

and they thought the black man was

threatening their lives

so they said hey we'll shoot a bullet back but actually

that plus 89 guess that's

what Hammurabi's code meant when it said an

eye for an eye

investigative unit found a firearm in his car

but couldn't tell if it was loaded?

officers couldn't stand to just remove the magazine or check the

barrel because of the time they'd already devoted

unarmed black man, 25 was killed by the police

is how the news sugarcoated

he wasn't just killed;

he was profiled, haunted, followed, pursued, and imploded

8 officers firing, 90 rounds.

if they ever did things equally that's more than 11 bullets each

when was a good time to stop pulling the trigger

and acknowledge Jayland Walkers defeat?

was he still a threat when he was empty handed

and stumbling, unable to stay on his feet?

anyone ready to cease fire

when he was laying on the

ground, motionless, appearing to be asleep?

local law enforcement not hearing our voice

so protests and rioting seem to be the only way

the City of Akron got scared and cancelled celebrations for

Independence Day

Oh well! we still gon' riot because that's not our holiday anyway

I tried to be nice but now that they not indicted

imma say all I gotta say

police force saying public trust is the biggest part of the problem

but tell me why I should trust them

if they don't even respond to danger when I call 'em

and when they have conflicts with black people,

bullets is how they solve em

they pledge allegiance to that badge

like the image of cops is awesome

by the way cops, I hear random things too,

just not regarding the situation

like you, I feel unreasonably threatened too, on occasion

voices in my head tell me the system is out to get me

and I'm not safe in my nation

and that the cops can kill me

and get away with it...

but wait, that's not my imagination...

#SAYMYNAME ELIJAH MCCLAIN

#SAYMYNAME ELIJAH MCCLAIN

Tonight I did something that wasn't so easy

I went out to the store alone and freely.

Or so I thought

I had my mask on to calm my anxiety

And someone in the neighborhood was secretly eyeing me

And for some odd reason the cops felt the need to quiet me

Walking home from the store with tea

Made me look shady so they stopped me

And just like George Floyd I said I couldn't breathe

I'm guessing since I was black they had to kill me,

but hey I guess it's better than hanging from a tree

"I can't breathe. I have my ID right here.

My name is Elijah McClain. That's my house.

I was just going home. I'm an introvert.

I'm just different. That's all.

I'm so sorry. I have no gun.

I don't do that stuff.

I don't do any fighting.

Why are you attacking me?

I don't even kill flies.

I don't eat meat!

But I don't judge people,

I don't judge people who eat meat.

Forgive me.

All I was trying to do was become better.

I will do it. I will do anything.

Sacrifice my identity.

I'll do it. You all are phenomenal.

You are beautiful. And I love you.

Try to forgive me. I am a mood Gemini.

I'm sorry. I'm so sorry.

Ow, that really hurt. You all are very strong.

Team work makes the dream work...(crying)...

oh I'm sorry. I wasn't trying to do that.

I just can't breathe correctly. (vomiting)

You see Elijah was known as a very peaceful person

to everyone who knew him and he taught himself

how to play the guitar and the violin

and he was nice enough that he'd play it for the stray kittens

Elijah didn't eat meat, because he thought all lives mattered

So much that he didn't kill flies,

and he brought joy to a room. And laughter.

Elijah was just unique, he wanted to change the world one

day, and if anyone would try to argue

he'd just say "I love you" and

walk away.

But the cops couldn't do it, they just couldn't have faith

that some of us are good, at least good enough to stay.

So they gave him drugs that caused more pain

and then imitated the chokehold that

they put him in, like it was a game.

So don't stop protesting, say his name

Rest in Peace,

Arrest the cops that killed Elijah McClain!

I RUN WITH AHMAUD

I RUN WITH AHMAUD

Justice For Ahmaud

Yeah... you guessed it, this is another black poem

But wait, don't leave. You need to hear this.

I mean, you're right, how dare I even come near this?

No, HOW DARE YOU try to clear this?

This is exactly why our black men fear this.

2 months later and they're just now in jail

Just because he wanted to jog on a trail

He was one out of 21 million black males

But he took in his last breath and never got to exhale

This is definitely a moment going down in history,

but I bet you his-story was different.

You say he was robbing houses, I don't care if he did or he didn't

That don't give you the right to be killin God's melanin children

He had to be a criminal because he fit the description

But here's the facade

Greg and Travis McMichael's said they were Christians

That they believe in God

But Romans 10:12 says that the Lord is Lord of all

Bestowing his riches on all those who call

Ephesians 2:14 God brought peace to us forever

He broke down the walls, and brought us together

and the most simple one; love thy neighbor

Instead of "Shoot first, Worry Later"

But to them he was, just another black kid

He was probably loud and probably ratchet, right?

What does it take for my brothers not to die tonight?

Trust and believe if my brothers die trynna fight for their lives

I won't be going down without a fight

I want our black people to stop dying

I want our black families to stop crying

I want these white men to stop Lying

So don't ask "What do you want from us? We're trying"

It's a citizens arrest, you ain't have to pull out a gun

It's a citizens arrest you not recording for fun

How would you feel if this happened to your all American son?

I want justice for Sandra bland. And justice for Trayvon

So I... I run with Ahmaud.

And I don't even run.

RELATIONSHIPS

BUILD BACK BETTER

BUILD BACK BETTER

This not the end, this can't be it for us

we don't need separation, we need time... and a little trust

we need to drop all our doubts & fears and leave 'em in the dust

because we deserve to be happy & enjoy our lives, and plus

we got plans for the future. To get married, have a house, & kids

so to the obstacles we can skip through & say it is what it is

we don't need to start over but we need to build better,

build our relationship off God

because through him, all things work together

infatuation is temporary, God is forever

and his unconditional love that expires, never,

tomorrow not promised so let's start today

let's repent, get on our knees, fold our hands & pray

that our weak foundation is eroded away

and let the father be the potter & mold us like clay

people say every kiss begins with K,

but every real relationship begins with J

So let's not follow the people, let's go by what the bible say

love is patient, love is kind

You got your patience, I'm working on mine

It is not jealous & does not brag

I wanna achieve our goals together & I'm not jealous.

I admire your swag

It does not dishonor others, and is not self seeking

We can't be selfish and only worry about how

WE'RE being treated

Love is "I make sure I'm okay, but still focus on you

So I can analyze my love from your point of view"

It is not quick to anger, and keeps no record of wrongs

So no quick temper and no holding grudges for long

Love does not delight in evil but rejoices in the truth

So no doing things in the dark,

although we're still members of youth

It always protects, always trusts, always hopes, always perseveres

Our love can get there, it's been partially there for a year

Verse 8 says love never fails

As long as we go by scripture, it won't fail I can tell

All we need is a bible built foundation

And a repentance prayer to get rid of our reputation

We can do this

CONFESSIONS OF A TEENAGE RELATIONSHIP

CONFESSIONS OF A TEENAGE RELATIONSHIP

This is not easy to say out loud because

I wanna keep it to myself

But I guess I gotta pull this book off the shelf

I wish I could tell you someway else

But I gotta do what I gotta do with the cards I was dealt

I love the way you think and I love the way you play

and I love the way you conduct yourself every single day

I love the way you work and I love the way you grind

and I love the way you control what's on your mind

I love the way you love, although it may sound selfish

But I love the way you care and I can't help it

I love how you act when you don't care who's around

and I love how you're the most handsome young man in town

You say my smile brightens your day, but how you think it got that way?

You see my smile when you bring it with the little things you do and say

I love your goofy demeanor and your happy spirit

and the joy that I can feel in your voice even when no one else can hear it

I love your patience and the way you understand

and how you provoke me to do what I can

I don't love you because you love me or how you make me feel

But I love how much I want us to have a future for real

Tupac said "forever isn't forever" but my love wouldn't die, ever

I love spending time with you. I love when we're together

and I love how you open your mind and retain information like

your head was severed. I love how your laughter

lights up anything going on in my head

and how you got determination to go out and get this bread

and how you're my motivation to get up and get out the bed

and how you want us to go to the top, and not stay down instead

I love how you're honest with me about the way you feel

and I love that God loves you and will help you heal

I found love in you and there's nothing, anybody can do

I wanna be in your life until it's through

And I wanna do it right, stand at the altar and say "I do"

Ouu this is why I love you

CONFESSIONS OF A TEENAGE BREAKUP

CONFESSIONS OF A TEENAGE BREAKUP

I knew this was going to end

It's like losing a love and my very best friend

I know it's for the best right now, but it still really hurts

I tried everything in my power just to make it work

and not having the closure I need, makes me feel worse

So I took a hot shower to calm me, then got tears on my new shirt

I don't know whether to cuss at you or thank you right now

I'm not sure if I should hug you or shank you right now

I get that you had to end things because it was damaging my health

But now I can't even think straight, I'm not myself

The me that I've gotten used to is so attached to you

And now that I don't have you, I don't know what to do

We had plans for a future. A house and some kids

But since we're still young, we gotta wait and say "it is what it is"

What about all the memories we shared

All the music and poetry I wrote about how much I care

Most teenagers would be suicidal and say they're ready to die

But that's not a desire of mine

I'm not ready to give up on life

I just need to know that when the time is right,

I'll get to be your wife Your sister told me what don't break us

makes us stronger So I'm trying to find out if this broke us or if

we'll be together longer That's another thing, the connection of our

families. The first person asking me if I'm okay was my best friend,

your brother, spamming me and my little sister-in-law whose

birthday was the very next day. Or my blood cousins who vouched

for our relationship in every way. Two months ago I was worried

about us going to sleep on the phone and now I gotta think about

dropping your stuff off at your moms home. Although I know

you're doing this for good, I'm still angry, hurt, upset, sad.

Because you left me banking on forever and I can't have that

Like how could you do this right when you were supposed to meet

my dad

And somehow, because you're my first love,

I still want you back

The only thing keeping me sane and stopping me from

losing my mind

Is the fact that this was just a case of the right person,

wrong time Who knows?

When everything has changed we probably

WILL get back together

Then we can get married and have our forever

But for now I don't wanna cry over you no more

My eyes so puffy and my head so sore

Maybe I shouldn't look at it as you left me,

just up and out the door

But maybe should look at this as an

opportunity to see what this

alone time has in store

My emotions all over the place

after the ending of that year

But soon enough, we'll be good and

I'll be okay, but for now we're here

CONFESSIONS OF A TEENAGE BREAKUP:
ONE YEAR LATER

It's been a year now and so much has changed

the love I have for you isn't the same

it's actually kinda crazy I felt that way in the first place

but there's nobody to blame

I would've given it all for you, where was my brain?

I said I loved this and that about you

when really all I loved who you seemed like from

my point of view all the stuff you said you were

and could be just wasn't true

like "I can give you the world" something you

could never do

"I can be the best husband" something you

could never be

how were you gonna be a good husband when you were

lying and cheating on me?

you drained me emotionally and therefore mentally

or did you think that was okay, maybe?

I'm so glad I dodged a bullet being your girlfriend

I don't get why I was so sad when

I knew it was going to end

but all teenagers have at least one heartbreak

so I had to take it on the chin

I thought you broke up with me for my health,

then found out you lied again when we were

trying to do the right thing you

were sneaking around then I found out you

had done some inappropriate things way back when

all in all I realized that you weren't a good person

but enough about the breakup,

lemme tell you how I been

I stopped lying about you

so I got closer with my mother

and for my health,

I distanced myself from your whole family,

even your toxic brother

I went to counseling and let it out and

started to feel content

I decided to let go of all the worthless time

and effort I spent

I brought up my grades and focused more on my future

and I created my own standards

so I don't end up with a loser

I got my privileges back because

I stopped breaking the rules

and I turned 15 obviously and yeah my

birthday was cool I got a job over the summer

so I could provide for me. So I won't depend on a

boyfriend to supply my needs.

I played soccer in the fall so I could stay in shape

and I got real cute for Homecoming

and that was great.

I made the basketball team

and became co-captain

and I'm allowed to have Instagram now

so I'm sure you saw that, and my raw caption.

I'm happy this far and it's been almost a year

but a lot of teenagers yearn for closure and in

case you do; here

I never wanna get back together, that typa love is gone

I hope someday you find a girl who loves you and she can

be the one

but first I'm hoping you'll get the help you need

I hope you'll start to see the problem I see

so maybe soon you'll got to therapy

and you won't scar another girl and leave her damaged like

you did me I pray you seek God and find him, nonetheless

and although you didn't treat me well,

I wish you the best

HALLMARK
MOMENTS

IN TIMES OF GRIEF

IN TIMES OF GRIEF

Praying for you in times

of hurt, pain and grief

Hoping that you're getting better

and that God is bringing you peace

I hope your sadness turns into joy and

I pray your worry turn into relief.

While you're not the best mentally,

I hope your eyes are open to see

That God is here to heal you and to help and so are we.

60 YEARS OF FAMILY

60 YEARS OF FAMILY

Cheers to family

What is family?

Family is the group of people you do the most with

Family is the group of people you get real close with

Family is the group of people you're found cheesin

in a Facebook post with and Family is the group of

people you make toasts with

So let's make a toast to our family right now

Cheers to those who made a life outside of

Cleveland and those who stuck around

To our beautiful melanin family

who are all different shades of brown

and cheers to Cousin Sharon's 60th and

celebrating in her hometown

1 decade for the natural hair

that nobody can rock like you

Another decade for the basketball skills and how

nobody can shoot score or hop like you

1 decade for the effort into the sign language fluency

Another decade for the passion for family unity

1 decade for the loyalty in friendships

Another decade for your belief that prayer is endless

Sixty is a milestone that many do not see

So every smile is a thank you for her soul that HE keeps

We've watched her learn lessons from those we have lost

And she carries forward Pearls lovely face,

and Aunt Dorothy's Sauce

Now for this celebration let's all raise a glass

For 60 more years toward the future and

60 years that have passed

Let's enjoy ourselves and all have a laugh

Because we never know what moment will be our last

F is for family and friends that are close to the fam

A is for the aunts and uncles that bring food in a big pan

M is for the mothers who work the hardest in every way

I is for in Gramma's backyard where she got down
every year on her birthday

L is for Lake Erie and the Cleveland sign for photos

Y is for your 60th birthday and your celebration and yolo

REMEMBER THE TIME

REMEMBER THE TIME

Here's a cheers to cousin VJ

On her sixty fifth bday

She's always SO selfless but it's her "today I'm celebrating me day"

we say happy birthday today and we just gone name it "V" Day, okay?

We all know Valerie's love for Michael Jackson

so tonight gon' be what it should be

We gonna "feel that beat, and we gone ride the boogie"

We gon' surely share some stories and some laughs,

and bring up everything funny

Because cousin Valerie's so joyful she can STILL enjoy some Bugs Bunny

So I heard Valerie used to send birthday cards

in the mail but I love that she send mine through technology

And back in the day you could experience that

same warmth walking into UH Radiology

Bringing her education from Central State,

y'all know she always shout 'em out

and you would also see that sweet smile

she has, and how her nails always poppin, I mean look at 'em right now

Cousin I want you to enjoy tonight so much,

more than you ever thought you would,

and dance so hard and so long, more than you thought you

could

Let's have some food and some cake, and celebrate a ton.

Experience all our family here and those that couldn't come

Valerie tap into your smoove personality like Cousin Darrell

would've done

Or get on down on the dance floor like Gramma Dorothy

when she was having fun

Valerie, I know you'll honor Aunt Pearl and be thankful

that you made it to sixty fine and know she's looking down

so proud every time she's on your mind

So think back on when she made your birthdays special and

made you feel so divine

and when you get overwhelmed with joy tonight, just like

Michael be blessed to just

"Remember the Time"

MOTHERS DAY 2021

MOTHERS DAY 2021

Shout out to the mothers

All of them, no exceptions

Got a harder job than others

No question

They work at work during the day

And work at home during the night

They gotta make sure they get paid

So the kids can eat right

They get money to spend it

on kids wants and needs

So when she said she loves you she meant it

Think about all her motherly deeds

When you went outside as a kid

And scraped your arm or your knee

How she cleaned out your scar

And wrapped it up with a Band-Aid

Or when she taught you how to drive a car

Or shared with you her lemonade

See I bet that made you smile

Because I brought up a memory

So go make your mom smile

Remind her of that imagery

Give something back to her

Because she gave life to you

and appreciate her

Because from her point of view

You're a blessing to her life

Something to give her all to

Even when you guys fight

She still loves you

Show her you love her today and all days

and if your mom's no longer here

Still celebrate the years

That you had with her

and all the good times that occurred

She's looking down on you and smiling

At the miracle she raised

With God she's flying

and with you she's amazed

Happy Mother's Day

HBCU TOUR II

HBCU TOUR II

From the beginning to the end

I learned so much and made some friends

We fit together like a puzzle despite our differences

One big happy family and W[inning] experiences

Now I know who I am and what I wanna do

I love you Ultimate HBCU Tour Two

ACKNOWLEDGEMENTS

I would like to thank my family for their
consistent unwavering support.
Mr. Basheer Jones for believing in me,
and GLB Publishing House for bringing my ideas to life.

And as always,
thank God for giving me the strength
to write through my pain in order to keep me sane.

Made in the USA
Columbia, SC
10 January 2024

30223075R00072